COMPLIMENTS OF
CASIMIR A. YOST

I am enclosing a copy of *America's Place in the World*, a
monograph prepared for the Institute for the Study of Diplomacy
and the Cox Foundation by U.S. Foreign Service Officer Daniel
R. Russel. Russel's essay critically examines the domestic and
international forces and concepts that shape American foreign
policy and offers valuable insights into how we should go about
undertaking our leadership role. I am sure you will find it useful
in understanding the complexities of the turn-of-the-century
foreign affairs scene.

America's Place in the World

We are grateful to the Una Chapman Cox Foundation for providing the financial support that made the publication and distribution of this report possible.

America's Place in the World

Daniel R. Russel

Institute for the Study of Diplomacy
EDMUND A. WALSH SCHOOL OF FOREIGN SERVICE
GEORGETOWN UNIVERSITY

Note: Daniel R. Russel is a State Department Foreign Service officer. The views and opinions expressed in this report are solely his and do not necessarily reflect those of the State Department.

Institute for the Study of Diplomacy
Edmund A. Walsh School of Foreign Service
Georgetown University, Washington, D.C.   20057–1025
© 2000 by the Institute for the Study of Diplomacy.

ISBN 0-934742-95-2
Printed in the United States of America

I join with you most cordially in rejoicing at the return of peace. I hope it will be lasting, and that mankind will at length, as they call themselves reasonable creatures, have reason and sense enough to settle their differences without cutting throats; for, in my opinion, there never was a good war or a bad peace. What vast additions to the conveniences and comforts of living might mankind have acquired if the money spent in wars had been employed in works of public utility? What . . . might have been obtained by spending those millions in doing good which in the last war have been spent in doing mischief.

—Benjamin Franklin, letter to Joseph Bank

Contents

Foreword

Challenged by a world that has lost its moorings? Adrift in complexities? Wondering why we don't have a simple, straightforward foreign policy? Many of us are; but one of us at least has taken time to think about it and write an analytical, thoughtful review of where we Americans now are in the world community, where we ought to be going, and why.

Mr. Russel's excellent essay on the post–Cold War world contains many valuable insights. In the face of today's complex international scene—which he documents brilliantly and with a sense of humor—he points out that there is no new universal field theory of diplomacy to replace the "predictability" of the Cold War. In fact, as Mr. Russel realizes, the "we" and "they" simplicities for which some seem to yearn were never so simple for those of us who struggled during the Cold War. Some states took advantage of the competition to better the offers for themselves from the two sides. Others had goals and objectives far removed from the competition, even as they tended to get caught up in it. As for predictability and simplicity, that too bears the scrutiny and careful analysis that history will inevitably bring.

What is fascinating about Russel's first-rate assessment is the number of clear insights into domestic policy motivations for U.S. leadership and our role in the "new world." Underlying the entire piece is a sense that our "interests," now more broadly defined, still form the basis for U.S. foreign policy in the post–Cold War world. None of us should be surprised; this has been the central stuff of foreign policy since people and leaders felt they needed one.

What is new is what now shapes our interests. To be sure, traditional security, economic prosperity, and our citizens' well-being at home and abroad remain at the core of our agenda. But there are new, global issues—health, environment, narcotics, terror, crime, and nuclear weapons proliferation—that are changing how we approach our security and well-being. New media influences also shape the reality and perception of our national interests. The "CNN factor" and the Internet, bringing us regional conflicts and natural calamities, live, in color, and in our living rooms, mold public opinion, which is felt rapidly in Washington. What the newspapers report, and how (!), also influences Washington's view and actions. Mr. Russel reaches some interesting conclusions about the consequences of the "real-time" information world for the conduct of U.S. foreign policy.

The essay also breaks new ground by drawing foreign policy analogies from the sociological theme of the "unrepaired broken windowpanes" (which lead to a decline in a neighborhood) and the epidemiological concept of the "tip-over point" (when a spate of disease turns into an epidemic). These creative and compelling parallels make for fascinating reading and invite further study.

Drawing on history, Mr. Russel ponders the ups and downs of U.S. public interest in foreign affairs and why the public, even when energized, fails to spur Congress to devote more attention and resources to foreign affairs. Why does the congressional leadership feel free to "dis" a subject that can shape the livelihood of 30 percent or more of their constituents? Perhaps we can draw an analogy to the consumer revolution. Until consumers got together as such, they were just taxpayers, employers, laborers, or farmers. Joined together, they became a powerful force. A similar synthesis among foreign policy supporters could have a similar multiplier.

Without such synergy and congressional support, funding for foreign policy will continue to flag. We are in real danger of turning on its head Winston Churchill's lend-lease dictum, "Give us the tools, and we will finish the job." It will soon become "Give us the job, and we will finish the tools." Without the resources, the tools, our national interests in foreign policy are unattainable. The danger to all of us should be obvious. Sadly, it is not

In part, this is because of our size. Continental states—Russia, India, China, the United States—look inward. Home is so big that what is happening there tends to consume any possible outward interests. New Jersey looks at New York, not Canada, Mexico, or

Europe. On the other hand, Belgium considers Benelux, the European Union, France, and NATO [the North Atlantic Treaty Organization] as daily drivers of interest. Belgians cannot afford not to learn English. Americans almost never master French, Spanish, or German, to say nothing of Russian, Chinese, Arabic, or Flemish. Our apparent cultural "self-sufficiency" is another reason why we are so cantankerously negative in Peoria or on Capitol Hill about foreign policy pursuits.

To sum up, in a complex world where no single theory of diplomacy prevails, U.S. leadership remains critical to international stability, security, democracy, and prosperity. However, America's complex political culture makes it hard to galvanize the public and congressional support for consistent, forthright leadership. It is in our national interest to find a way to focus the widespread but poorly organized public involvement in international affairs, translating it into the resources and tools required for continued U.S. leadership in the world. Russel's essay is one of the first genuine efforts to put all of these pieces together in a coherent and engaging fashion. It should be required reading for anyone interested in foreign affairs—professional, amateur, university student, think tanker, business person, or "NGOer [nongovernmental organization]." It is remarkably well written and a significant contribution to thinking about our role in the world around us today, tomorrow, and on into the next century.

Thomas R. Pickering
Under Secretary for Political Affairs
Department of State

Introduction

I originally wrote this paper during a sabbatical as a report to the trustees of the Una Chapman Cox Foundation in early 1997 but had to put it aside for over two years when recalled to the State Department. Thanks to the Institute for the Study of Diplomacy at Georgetown University, I was able to review and revise it during the summer of 1999. I hope that the worst of the anachronisms have been removed, leaving the observations that appear to have withstood the test of those thirty months.

There were two aspects to the paper that particularly struck me upon rereading. First and foremost was the profound effect of the sustained period of U.S. economic good health, which had significantly diluted the lingering sense of anxiety (occasionally bordering on xenophobia) that I encountered in 1996. The lack of impact on the United States of the collapse of the Thai baht in 1997, which triggered the "Asian financial crisis," which in turn infected other economies such as Brazil, effectively undermined the growing sense of American declinism. The notion that America's halcyon days were behind us and that we were fated to go the ignominious way of all empires was muscled aside by the heroically robust growth of the U.S. economy. No longer did the trend lines appear to preview an anemic U.S. economy in whose face EU [European Union] and Asian bullies would kick sand. By the same token, the defiant challenge of "Asian values," fueled by a dogma of self-sufficiency, yielded ignominiously to pleadings and promises in return for help from the IMF [International Monetary Fund].

A second observation pertains to my fears about Congress. The midterm congressional election of '94 and the Republican revolution

1

that it represented and precipitated appeared to have spawned a trend toward neoisolationism or at least withdrawal. The early stages of the presidential campaign of '96 (at least until the collapse of Pat Buchanan's nativist primary challenge) combined with the shutdown of the federal government to suggest that Congress was cycling back toward the era of "know-nothingism" and "America First." Many of Congress's veterans in foreign affairs retired or were voted out, and the 104th Congress was replete with novices. This trend in fact continued; in the 106th Congress, for example, freshmen senators chair every subcommittee of the Foreign Relations Committee.

Despite this, and notwithstanding the unsatisfactory outcomes of so many congressional engagements in foreign affairs, the prophecies of a neoisolationist Congress have not been realized. Instead, many of the revolutionary freshmen of '94 have left, roughly one-quarter of them victims of electoral defeat, disillusionment, or term limits. Some of the newcomers have revealed an exceptional talent for international affairs. And, in fact, the administration and Congress were able to register some significant legislative accomplishments in international affairs such as NATO enlargement, IMF funding, and the Nunn-Lugar program for disposing of or safeguarding the nuclear weapons of the former Soviet Union. As regards foreign policy, the year 2000 presidential race today appears to be playing out on quite different terrain than the inhospitable landscape of the last one.

As these observations suggest, the scene appeared more bleak when I set out on a voyage of discovery in 1996. I resolved to use the Una Chapman Cox Fellowship to investigate a series of conundrums: an apparent resurgence of American isolationism at the peak of U.S. international authority and in a time of unprecedented global integration; a growing sense in the United States of economic nationalism despite the prevalence in U.S. economic life of imports, exports, and commercial multinationalism; and the American demand for results in international security matters combined with an absolute aversion to military risks.

The question that seized my attention was how Americans think the United States fits into the world, what it meant to them to be the world's lone "superpower," and why there was an apparent prevalence of declinism and fatalism about America's prospects. This led me to ask if there is something intrinsic to the American creed that helps explain U.S. behavior and predilections. Are today's Americans as a people fated to pursue idealistic goals—the export of democracy, human rights, and self-determination—and to reject the pragmatic realpolitik of their political ancestors?

Measuring attitudes toward such a thing as "internationalism" is an imprecise business. Statistically, I found that, by and large, the baseline ratio of 65:30 in favor of an active role in world affairs has held remarkably consistent over the years. It soon became clear, however, that the statistics mask dramatic twists and turns in attitudes about *how* Americans view and think the United States should deal with the world. I looked at where Americans placed emphasis in international affairs, based on my assumption that the world is relevant to people in terms of their particular interests and their concerns, not as an abstraction or as pertaining to civic duty. Surveys suggested concerns about protecting jobs, about drugs, and about nuclear proliferation. At the same time, there was remarkable indifference toward the goals of proselytizing such national values as human rights and democracy or helping others, whether it be to fend off aggression or famine. And yet, as the 1991 Gulf War showed, however much energy security may have factored in the equation, people *will* rally around a principle they do not pay much mind to in the abstract. When President George Bush declared in 1991 that "we went halfway around the world to do what is moral, just and right," he was telling Americans something that they very much wanted to hear.

There are strong historical and sociological bases for explaining Americans' relatively modest interest in world affairs, I found, but the claim that isolationism is enshrined in their very makeup is far from the truth. I discovered that historical and sociological factors have made it virtually impossible to successfully conduct realpolitik along traditional European lines, in part because of the multicultural makeup of the nation and in part because of popular moralism with respect to U.S. foreign policy despite the lack of support for proselytizing American values abroad.

I looked at the very credible theory that a combination of factors flowing from the increasingly complex environment was negatively affecting foreign policy. First among these was the ignorance of the U.S. public about the world. Second, the rise of single issue pressure groups as well as the emergent influential role of nongovernmental organizations (NGOs). Third, the frequently partisan and interventionist character of Congress (quick to resort to legislation on lesser issues). And fourth, a complex and convoluted executive branch bedecked with ever-more specialized agencies and task forces.

I was gradually convinced instead that in fact the public—although it could be very wrong on specific issues in the short term—was impressively sound in its long-term judgments about what was important or what was wrong in American foreign policy. I found evidence to support what political scientists call "low-information rationality"—the ability to apply common sense and rules of thumb to issues about which people possess rather modest amounts of knowledge—and became convinced that popular democratic involvement in the shaping of foreign policy is indeed the "worst system except for all the rest." Moreover, the principle of rational prioritizing—i.e., that people care about foreign policy issues to the extent that the issues are germane to their lives—provided a better framework for understanding the relationship between domestic and foreign affairs than the prevalent model of zero-sum competition in the world and at home.

Next, my research led through the proliferation of theories produced in the search for a new paradigm to replace Cold War containment as an organizing principle for international affairs. This invited an attempt to inventory some of the important changes evident after the Cold War, which in turn revealed many developments that, while profound, were causally unrelated to it. The spike in popular cynicism and mistrust of government, so vivid in the '94 and '96 campaigns, was one such shift. The transforming effect of the media/communications revolution was another. This latter change, I found, plays a paradoxical role in that transparency both begets and reveals deceptiveness on the part of leaders. At the same time that the selection bias of the media favors bad news, efforts to spin stories (rather than to explain and persuade) reinforce cynical public views of government.

In these jaunts through competing paradigms, I encountered, and took issue with, the several guises of a doctrine of "vital national interests" that struck me as essentially representing a kind of modern feudalism. This includes the notion that the United States must limit its scope to select core concerns and let the "periphery" fend for itself. Overly zealous application of the principle of national interest took several forms: modesty, fatigue, and self-interest. Some argued that the U.S.'s role is more suitably that of "first among equals" and that we must reconcile ourselves to a world of regional powers dominating spheres of influence. Some asserted that the burdens of leadership are too heavy and that other nations across the globe must step up to assume more responsibilities. Others maintained that the United States must act unilaterally in defense of its "real" interests, unconstrained by multilateral liens on its sovereignty.

The conclusion that presented itself to me was that the preservation of U.S. dominion is both possible and highly desirable. As the largest "equity" holder in planet Earth, we have a vital national interest in maintaining a degree of order and worldwide adherence to norms that deters malefactors and reduces the need for emergency intervention. I find applicable models in the epidemiological concept of the "tipping point"—the threshold of disorder where a confinable outbreak of illness becomes an unstoppable epidemic. The theories of "order maintenance" and crime control were germane. The thesis of "broken windows"—namely that people behave more responsibly in an ordered environment—suggests that American investment in international affairs can significantly reduce the likelihood and extent of future U.S. involvement in serious crises. In other words, the beat cop who knows his community and involves himself in its affairs is far more effective in deterring crime than is the high-tech, high firepower, rapid response SWAT team sent in to combat it.

In examining the prevailing prescriptions for the United States in the post–Cold War world, I found a chronic confusion between power—particularly, military power—and leadership. Military strength is a necessary but insufficient basis for the United States to exercise authority in the world. The United States must have and be seen to have the wherewithal to defend itself, its allies, and its interests and to coerce others when necessary. Overwhelming military strength contributes immeasurably to national prestige and deters potential challengers from embarking on an effort to catch up, thereby avoiding future arms races. But it is wholly insufficient, for two distinct sets of reasons. First, because the cost to the United States for using force is often prohibitively high, both in domestic terms (i.e., blood and money) and in the consequences to our relations with other nations. Secondly, and more importantly, because the exercise of authority entails motivating others to act willingly without resort to coercion. Our national interest—indeed, our vital national interest—lies in cultivating an international environment that is inimical to conflict and supportive of the orderly resolution of problems. In that context, multilateral diplomacy can serve as a significant multiplier of American influence as well as a utilitarian vehicle for mitigating state-to-state conflict.

I concluded that because international affairs require the United States to take account of factors such as ethnicity, NGOs, international agencies, multinational corporations, and the media, and because of the proliferation of transnational or global issues, we require more diplomatic involvement, not less. The Ross Perot canard that a president can get by with CNN and a fax machine is debunked simply by the volume of news conveyed by modern electronic media, the relentless pressure for quick action, and the inevitable replay abroad of pronouncements aimed at the domestic audience. The United States continues to need the capacity to monitor, evaluate, and influence the behavior of other nations so that without coercion they will act in ways that are at least consistent with U.S. interests and values.

Not only must the United States be informed, it must be unified and coherent. Discord between the executive and legislative branches undermines the solidarity and predictability of American foreign policy. The Hill, often dissatisfied with administration policies, has attempted to apply legislative techniques to an unruly world through a proliferation of laws intended to prescribe policies and punishments for international behavior. Lawyerly tools are unsuited to managing relations among states. Some laws have produced unintended negative consequences; others have carried such draconian penalties that the administration has found it difficult to implement them. The absolutism of legislated foreign policy contributes to the perception of America as arrogant and dictatorial. Efforts to safeguard against utopian hyperactivism—both by restricting funds and applying strictures against "nonvital" interventions—are misplaced. No single, abstract principle of involvement will accommodate every situation. More importantly, we cannot look into the seeds of conflict and say which grain will grow and which will not. Any policy that stipulates dealing only with emergencies is guaranteed to provide an endless supply of them.

It becomes clear that there is inevitably a mix of factors governing American involvement in or neglect of an international issue, above and beyond the philosophy of a particular administration. One factor is strategic: self-defense, protecting U.S. borders, promoting economic prosperity, etc. Another is political: either international (assisting allies, meeting obligations) or domestic (responding to media, interest group, grassroots, or old-fashioned political pressure). The sway of American values, traditions, and biases can be considerable in foreign policy-making. There are also practical considerations such as the natural priority accorded to problems in close proximity over distant ones or the logistical considerations related to intervention. Lastly, there is the influence of the foreign policy establishment who identify problems, advise leaders, and plan, react, and carry out plans. Ideally, these professionals in the executive branch serve as the regulator to get the mix right. Ultimately, a significant policy wobble will develop when they get it wrong.

The lesson here is that we must be polytheists in foreign policy. We cannot worship exclusively at the shrine of vital national interest, of political expediency, of human rights, of convenience and practicality, or even of technocracy and professionalism. Each of these elements must be recognized, understood, at times influenced or altered, and factored into the policy equation. The intended result is a purposeful foreign policy that aims at a world we can live in and moves toward that goal by synthesizing the diverse forces and competing considerations involved. The overpowering interest of the United States rests in using our wiles, wealth, and wisdom to create and preserve a peaceful world congenial to our values, not merely in staving off disaster when it is upon us. In the speech that President Franklin D. Roosevelt was to have delivered on 13 April 1945, the day after he died, he had written the following: "More than an end to war, we want an end to the beginnings of all wars."

1
Who Are We?

The Founders, as revolutionaries, were convinced that the United States had a special responsibility to spread its values and contribute to world peace, albeit by example, not by intervention. The belief in the moral superiority of the American form of government, and the notion of the civilizing mission that it produced, form the foundation for an activist, not an isolationist, foreign policy. George Washington's own philosophy contravenes the creed of many of those most fond of invoking his farewell address. Washington believed that, once the nation grew to the point that its security could not easily be threatened, the United States could turn to its greater ethical mission in the world. "It should be the highest ambition of every American to extend his views beyond himself and to bear in mind that his conduct [may] . . . influence . . . the world," he wrote in a letter. He believed that Americans should aspire to create a great nation, whose international conduct would exemplify justice and benevolence and, by imbuing its policies with moral content, would lead by example.

Realism—or realpolitik, to give it its appropriately foreign-sounding name—refers expressly to the international diplomacy of balance conducted on the basis of the assessed strength of the players without reference to moral principles or world opinion. Despite the adroitness of American colonial forebears in the actual practice of realpolitik (utilizing the French or British against the other to protect the interests of the new nation), the admonition against political entanglement and the conviction of U.S. exceptionalism clearly reflected their negative view of European "realism." The crucial tenet of realism—that the end justifies the means—contradicted the American emphasis on human freedom and dignity and contravened the

Jeffersonian precept that states be held to the same moral standards of conduct as individuals. The Founders thought that peace depended not on balancing power but on promoting democratic institutions.

Politics in a democracy is about what people think is right or, at a minimum, what their leaders can persuade them is right. Even as ardent a student of Metternich as Henry Kissinger and as calculating a politician as Richard Nixon could not succeed in carrying out their foreign policy goals in Southeast Asia. Kissinger wrote in *Diplomacy,* "The drawback of [our] approach was its dearth of emotional resonance among the American people." "Dearth of emotional resonance" may not be how many Americans remember the Vietnam years; a less delicate formulation might be that the American people insist on an animating vision and a persuasive moral underpinning to major foreign policy undertakings.

The great strength of the United States—some would argue its greatest—is the power of its principles, not that of its military or its economy. In the words of Arthur Schlesinger, "Ideals are an indispensable constituent of American power." The cleverest realpolitik simply cannot garner the support or command the moral authority that is inspired by the liberal democratic principles of the United States. Ideology proved powerful enough to end the Cold War confrontation long before the realists' "equilibrium" would have. The ideological factor, not simply power, drew economically advanced countries into the orbit of the United States and put the Soviets on the defensive, forcing them to build walls to keep people in and ideas out. The United States could justifiably claim that its interests were the world's interests because so much of the world subscribed to its basic values. Ultimately, the foment in Eastern Europe that broke the Soviet bloc's back was not a product of realpolitik so much as the alignment of its people with Western values and their rebellion against a system's failure to provide for their material and spiritual requirements.

Yet notwithstanding the pride that Americans seem to take in the spread of democracy, the consistent evidence of modern polls is that promoting American values rates at the bottom of the public's foreign policy agenda. Part of the explanation for the dichotomy lies in the difference between the way people respond to questions in the abstract and in the event. Media coverage of developments in the world activates a sense of moral outrage or lends a strong identification with an inspirational cause and overwhelms traditional strategic

foreign policy considerations. This flows from the fact that people prioritize concerns with reference to their own lives, current events, and
the international environment of the moment. Graphic media coverage of Tiananmen Square, the Gulf War, famine and genocide in
Africa, and the plight of refugees in the Balkans and evidence of ethnic cleansing repeatedly caused the American people to rally behind
principles to which they normally pay little heed in the abstract.
Moreover, it is in the nature of the U.S.'s outspoken and activist
democracy for citizens to organize to advocate their views. The
advent of cable TV, faxes, and the Internet has radically accelerated
this trend.

Despite the new media through which information is dissemi-
nated, the well-documented American ignorance of the world
remains breathtaking. Surveys highlight the grim statistics—for example, that Americans rank last among a dozen industrialized nations in
basic world knowledge. Whether or not the new sources of information have enhanced the American public's *ability* to make informed
judgments about foreign policy issues, they seems to promote the
public's *confidence* in its opinions about them. The trend is away from
deference to a foreign policy "elite" and toward a more egalitarian
environment in which everyone has an opinion on everything, and
anyone's opinion is as good as anyone else's. Unlike domestic and
economic matters, where people have reference points and reality
checks in their day-to-day lives, foreign affairs are by definition
remote. Because people have less direct experience and less interest
in foreign policy, their opinions are more general and more malleable.

In *American Exceptionalism*, Martin Lipset brilliantly described
the ills that flow from "the dark side" of the American creed: from
the emphasis on personal responsibility, independent initiative, and
activism come selfishness, litigiousness, and a disregard for the common good. The moralism that produces patriotism as well as antiwar
movements also generates a vindictive moral absolutism that bars
compromise. The American creed is highly individualistic, antistate,
and laissez-faire. This is reflected in an American bias against government aid or welfare. The United States is the most philanthropic
nation in terms of personal, religious, and corporate giving but the
stingiest among industrialized nations in terms of social welfare. No
industrialized nation gives proportionately less in foreign aid or more
in private donations. As Will Rogers quipped, "American diplomacy is
an open book—a check book." Poll after poll shows that Americans

are erroneously convinced that the United States gives proportionately more aid than any other nation. Some 60 percent of Americans polled said they favored "lowering" the level of foreign aid to 5 percent of the federal budget, a step that would constitute a 500 percent increase in the actual amount spent!

Despite the low standing of advocacy for spreading American values, politicians are presumably responding to something real when they feel compelled to reaffirm their commitment to defend and propagate these principles throughout the world. Foreign policies have political ramifications at home, just as politics can often drive foreign policies. An effective politician must manage both the issues and the symbols. Thus it is not enough for a leader to make a practical case to constituents for a given policy (e.g., doing business with China); he must also reconcile the policy with the symbolic image of America (e.g., champion of human rights). George Kennan, in his classic review of American diplomacy, bemoaned what he called the extreme political self-consciousness of American diplomacy. A given statement or action will be rated a triumph in Washington if it is popular in domestic political circles (i.e., the intended audience) even if it is ineffective or even self-defeating in terms of its external effects. When this is carried to extremes, Kennan complained, American diplomacy tends to degenerate into a series of postures struck with only secondary consideration given to its actual effect.

That nexus between domestic politics and foreign policy no longer plays out along the axis of the Cold War. Moreover, the traditional inclusive concept of American identity—the melting pot—has begun to yield to the image of a "mosaic"—the dogma of social solidarity—multiculturalism, which challenges "e pluribus unum" and rejects assimilation. There is nothing new about domestic interest groups influencing foreign policy, but multiculturalism has resulted in a growing intrusion of ethnicity into the foreign policy calculus. The United States has a constituency for and against virtually every issue, rivalry, feud, and grievance on Earth. The proliferation of interest groups, along with the enhanced effectiveness of their organizational and communications prowess, is today a significant factor in foreign affairs. Interest groups' importance has been magnified in the absence of the Cold War, during which the paramount struggle against Communism overshadowed or submerged most lesser issues.

The diversity and character of the United States present unique difficulties in defining a foreign affairs mission and in bringing people along. Internal fragmentation makes it harder to sell the idea of a unified national interest. National interest can look quite different to different groups. Natural champions of one cause are natural opponents of another. The same group of Hispanic Americans who vigorously support NAFTA [the North American Free Trade Agreement] and the Mexican peso bailout may be offended by policies aimed at stemming immigration, presenting a conundrum for policymakers. One can see a proliferation of foreign issues in which an ethnic constituency might play an influential, complicating role beyond the familiar cases of Cuba, Northern Ireland, and Israel. The diversity of our interests and goals also complicates the effort. For example, the requirements to safeguard human rights, shore up a fledgling democracy, discourage a regional military buildup, and improve leverage in bilateral relations may all lead toward contradictory conclusions in deciding on an arms transfer. Clarity of goals will never eliminate the need for leaders to make difficult judgments or pursue imperfect solutions to intractable problems.

In Congress, the policy-making trend has been away from the discipline of party and committee hierarchy and toward individualism among members. In the pre-Watergate era, the party or committee leadership would arrive at a position on a foreign affairs issue, either through negotiations with the administration or in party caucuses. Personal ideology or attachment to a given issue were irrelevant (except in regard to the committee or party leaders). Once a position was set, it was "whipped" down the line, and members by and large were expected to adhere to it. That structure steadily eroded through the 1980s and today, members of Congress have become virtually autonomous. It is no longer the renegade but now the average member who has his own positions or her own media operations and increasingly demands that the executive branch negotiate policy with him or her directly and individually. This diffusion of power provides entree and access for interest groups, which can compete with the administration to develop congressional support.

Another factor is the high turnover in Congress; more than two-thirds of the 106th Congress was elected after the fall of the Berlin Wall. This means that members, by and large, are decidedly inexperienced in matters of foreign affairs. There is a well-documented learning curve that shows only a slow shift in emphasis from local constituent concerns, which dominate the agenda of freshmen, to national affairs, which are of increased concern to long-time members. Self-imposed term limits, resignations, and electoral defeats have thinned the ranks of some of the archconservative freshmen from the class of '94. Even so, the profile of new members is changing in terms of their professional backgrounds and worldview. They are largely of the Vietnam generation (though rarely veterans), wary of "quagmires." They tend to be local thinkers, and proud of it.

Because this trend unfolds in an international affairs environment without the doomsday specter of nuclear confrontation with the Soviet Union, members perceive that little harm to national security will come of taking a position on foreign relations, whereas a position on domestic affairs can entail substantial gains or penalties in the next election. This gives greater primacy to the political dimension of an international problem and also consigns many foreign policy issues to horse-trading. Legislators can swap support on a foreign policy issue of importance to one constituency much as they have always done on local pork-barrel projects. The promotion of political advantage can trump good foreign policy if the fate of the free world is not seen hanging in the balance. Thus, one member's zealous support for a particular policy course on a lower profile issue—whether driven by ideology, staff activism, effective lobbying by foreign governments, or constituent pressure—can often garner congressional support and shape legislation (even over administration opposition).

When Congress resorts to legislation as a means of preventing or compelling action by administrations, a host of unwelcome consequences can follow. Issues between nations—intrinsically political—are recast in lawyerly terms. Other countries respond in kind, retaliating or passing laws aimed at nullifying the effect of U.S. legislation. The mechanistic structure of legislated sanctions supplants the art of negotiation, inhibits compromise, and leads to undesired outcomes. In some cases, legislation would force the United States to take punitive action without regard to the negative consequences that may follow. A law intended as a lever to push for better counternarcotics cooperation, might—if implemented—seriously disrupt bilateral cooperation in a host of other areas, lead to job losses at home, heighten tension in a region, and end such cooperation on illicit drugs as may have existed.

Since it falls to the administration to square the circle of legislative and real-world requirements, the executive branch will be tempted to work around the letter of the law even where it seeks to implement its spirit. Some combination of diplomatic collaboration with affected countries, loopholes in the legislation, and general obfuscation usually softens (or prevents) the application of the penalty in the law. This leads to vicious cycles: congressional frustration leads to legislated penalties that are both more draconian and evasion resistant; since legal sanctions are rarely applied, the drafters of legislation tend to think less of the consequences of new sanctions; the locus of debate shifts from potential solutions to politicized arguments over the application of the law.

On most issues, Congress is content to allow the executive branch to formulate and pursue its own policies without particular interference; binding legislative action is viewed as a course of last resort. If the administration appears to know what it is doing, and Congress knows what the administration is doing and why, the probability of legislation decreases. If bills and amendments are attention-getting devices, perhaps the answer is to devote more (or perhaps the right kind of) attention to the views and priorities on Capitol Hill. The executive branch's foreign policy establishment is notorious for poor relations with Congress. The primary mode of interaction—testimony by an administration official before a committee—is regarded as a gladiator sport by both sides. While no silver bullet, it seems clear that an administration that makes a virtue of early and extensive consultations with Congress as part of the process of clarifying goals and priorities will, in the long run, be accorded far greater latitude in foreign affairs.

There is no doubt that the President—particularly an articulate politician such as Bill Clinton—has tremendous power to communicate ideas and to shape public views, especially on foreign policy issues. The potency of presidential leadership is most conspicuous in times of national crisis, when the heroic qualities of the leader (e.g., Franklin D. Roosevelt) galvanize the nation or (in the case of Herbert Hoover) when they are absent. Ironically, the more prosaic (albeit complex) challenges of peacetime and plenty can make it harder for a President to innovate or to push controversial policies. If the status quo is comfortable and the Republic is safe, even the most charismatic President will face a challenge in pursuing ambitious programs. The executive branch has grown dramatically through the century and weathered repeated attempts at streamlining. This has not necessarily translated into greater clout, in part because much of the growth has been fragmentary and ad hoc. Sketched out in a diagram, the proliferation of White House offices, bureaus, councils, directorates, envoys, and presidential advisors looks less like a bureaucratic blueprint and more like a Rube Goldberg contraption

Foreign policy questions are routinely run through the gauntlet of the interagency process. This three-ring circus operates at the working level, at the so-called "deputies" (i.e., senior policy officials) level, and at the level of cabinet secretaries and agency heads. The regular players include the National Security Council, the State Department, the Defense Department (bifurcated into its civilian and uniformed components), the Central Intelligence Agency, the Vice President's staff, the Permanent Representative to the United Nations, the Department of the Treasury, the U.S. Agency for International Development, and—depending on the issues—can include the National Economic Council, Commerce, Justice (often with separate Federal Bureau of Investigation representation), the U.S. Trade Representative, the Office of Drug Control, and so on. The trend is toward separate representation for each facet of a problem and each point of view in policy councils. Nor is this fragmentation limited to Washington. Embassies abroad are increasingly used as platforms for the off-shore operation of Washington agencies. It is no longer unusual to find an aggregation of agencies—the Federal Aviation Administration, the Drug Enforcement Administration, the Federal Bureau of Investigation, the Secret Service, the Department of Agriculture, the Department of Commerce, the Department of Transportation, the Internal Revenue Service, the Immigration and Naturalization Service, etc.—operating out of an embassy. Regardless of the U.S. ambassador's mandate for oversight and coordination, the ease of independent, often secure communication fosters freelancing.

Even the ostensibly nonparochial agencies such as the State Department and the National Security Council, which are mandated to deal with all aspects of a problem, are themselves increasingly patchworks of specialized bureaus and directorates. The creation of the National Economic Council in the first Clinton administration was premised on the theory of a distinction between national economic and security interests that warranted a separate but equal coordinating mechanism. There is more at work in this trend than simply bureaucratic mitosis; the subdivision of agencies and the proliferation of specialized players are a direct function of the increased prominence of new (or belatedly recognized) issues. Global warming, after all, is no longer simply a meteorological function. Neither are narcotics, law enforcement, immigration, trade practices, or infectious diseases merely technical issues. It is no longer self-evident that terrorism is a police matter to be handled by agents with guns. The U.S. Coordinator for Counterterrorism must orchestrate the efforts of a dozen domestic and foreign affairs agencies, work with local sheriffs and foreign ministers, and be as expert in the threat from a computer virus as that from the anthrax virus. Added to this propagation of nontraditional executive branch actors with discrete agendas is the growth of the size, purview, and activism of the National Security Council itself, which—as the direct staff of an elected official—is not immune to constituent pressure and domestic political calculations.

In the same way that a national crisis can transform a President from the chief executive officer of the government apparatus to the commander in chief of the nation, a serious and well-defined external threat serves to unify the bureaucracy. Conversely, the absence of a major foe facilitates fragmentation in both government structure and government policy. Taken as a whole, the net result of these trends is that the requirements of managing and balancing domestic and international pressures and of making compromises and resolving disputes, while by no means new, are steadily moving international policy-making to resemble the patterns of politics at the local level. In dealing with foreign affairs, Presidents today increasingly must function like big city mayors—juggling the concerns and interests of various groups, engineering trade-offs, brokering compromises among rival ideologies, building coalitions, and at times perhaps pandering.

Is this the calamity of democracy against which the "realists" have long warned? In *Essays in the Public Philosophy,* Walter Lippman wrote, "Public opinion has been destructively wrong at critical junctures [and] impressed a critical veto on the judgments of informed and responsible officials. Mass opinion has acquired a mounting power in this country. It has shown itself to be a dangerous master of decision when the stakes are life and death." Lippman worried about the prospects for democratic government because the "spirit of Jacobism" had destroyed the proper balance between rulers and ruled, resulting in "excesses of democracy" and "derangements" that he asserted would result in the "catastrophic decline of Western society."

Political compromise and expediency are the prices paid by policymakers in a democratic system. The U.S. system is one of limited stewardship—leaders must answer to the people for their actions. Stern urgings to leave policy to the "experts" have never made a difference. In a democratic system, leaders maintain power by adopting policies that garner popular support. The alternative, leaving decisions to those who "know best," is fundamentally authoritarian.

The theory of a wise elite operating without the interference of politics is a myth. Public accountability and the vigorous political challenges that compel an administration to explain and justify its policies are essential safeguards. No one can improve on the observation of Winston Churchill that democracy is the worst form of government except for all the rest. The proposition that leaders know best what is right for their countries has been put to the test throughout history, with appalling results. Even Walter Lippman dramatically revised his view of the superiority of elite foreign policy management as a result of the conduct of the Vietnam War.

A number of analytic studies of popular opinion conclude that shifts in public attitudes have not been random, hysterical, or unreasonable. Despite the ignorance of the public in terms of factual knowledge about the world, public policy preferences shift—not in "mood swings"—but according to the "sensible citizen" pattern—that is, appropriately to significant events or meaningful shifts in political or economic circumstances. The conundrum of public ignorance on the one hand and "sensible judgment" on the other is described by the term "low information rationality." To the extent that public opinion is rational, it is because people are responding on the basis of what they in fact *do* know, not operating strictly from prejudice or partisanship. What people know and care about, of course, tends to be the things that affect them directly. Thus, it is fair to say that people tend to prioritize along natural and generally rational lines.

Therefore, while the public's agenda has domestic and foreign policy dimensions, it would be misleading to think in terms of two separate agendas. The baseline numbers for public support for international involvement (which have held remarkably steady throughout the second half of the twentieth century at about 65 percent in favor and 30 percent against) mask the constant churning of priorities. People continually recalibrate what they consider to be relevant. Since the end of the Cold War, public support has slipped for the traditional category of military security. Nevertheless, people are still concerned about safeguarding their surroundings. That means they want the government to act against the spread of weapons of mass destruction, combat terrorism, and prevent the destruction of the environment; they even want to utilize the United Nations to attain these priorities. Because people are concerned about society and their own welfare, their emphasis is on halting the flow of narcotics, protecting jobs, stemming illegal immigration, and advancing U.S. business interests abroad.

2
Diplomacy in a Real-Time World

There is a wonderful 1950s television skit in which Sid Caesar, dressed as a doughboy, perfectly captures historical anachronism by throwing his helmet in the air and shouting, "Hurrah! World War ONE is over!" We need Sid Caesar's comic genius to name this era. For the United States, certainly, the basic paradigm of the twentieth century has been the epochal, ideological, and sometimes Manichean struggle between American values and the enemy: the Huns, the Nazis, and the Communists. The fall of the Soviet Union quickly brought the recognition that the old paradigm no longer served and launched an inconclusive search for a new paradigm: a terse but generally applicable doctrine that can be used as a guide to check policy coordinates.

The theorem that history somehow ended with the demise of Communism flamed out quickly. None of the newly proffered principles—ideological, civilizational, geopolitical, or other—has proven durable. George Bush's "New World Order" proved to have a low content-to-rhetoric ratio and was quickly deflated. The Clinton administration's attempts to develop a formula with content, such as "assertive multilateralism" and "enlargement," were beset by attackers from virtually all political corners, even as their precepts were being challenged by events that stubbornly refused to validate the theses. This leaves us, to borrow Richard Haas's phrase, in "a period of 'international deregulation,' (colloquially known as 'The New Mess') in which there are new players, new capabilities, and new alignments—but, as yet, no certain new rules."

The Soviet threat made many of the "whys" of foreign affairs irrelevant. Today, in the multicultural, modern United States, even support for the Kurds in northern Iraq or criticism of South Africa's arms sales to Syria are controversial. The maxim "the enemy of my enemy is my friend" no longer holds in an environment in which enemies and friends can be difficult to distinguish. What potential foe does not have a vocal expatriate presence in the United States? Today, even allies of the United States are not necessarily friends when it comes to neuralgic issues such as trade with Cuba or Iran. Admittedly there was no shortage of disputes between the United States and its allies during the Cold War, but the past inhibition against divisions that could be exploited by the enemy is certainly missing today.

The glass is also half full. The competing ideologies of fascism, communism, and what might be called chauvinism (e.g., the pan-Arab state, the Islamic revolution, "Asian values") have each failed. There is now a broad—although by no means universal—international consensus in support of shared ideals, values, and normative principles relating to democracy, free markets, and human and civil rights. This is evident in the trend of common action and cooperation among core democratic states and in the progression of important transition states (e.g., Russia and China) that are moving along a trajectory toward reform and integration. The discrediting of defunct ideologies and the demonstrated porosity of borders combine to emphasize the points of commonality and common interest among nations. At the same time, those nations that opt out (or are excluded) are increasingly liable to failure.

Relentless economic competition in the world has bankrupted the principle of national self-sufficiency, gouged holes in the traditional economic defenses of nations, created transnational dependencies, and widened the gap between the technologically literate and the industrially challenged. Economically driven migratory pressures pump foreign workers into the labor pools of every developed nation at the same time as their economic elites are being integrated into global enterprises. The developed world has come to rely on an ultra-sophisticated but delicate infrastructure that is vulnerable to attack—terrorist, criminal, vandal, or psychotic. Non-national loyalties—religious, ethnic, tribal, and regional—are promoting alliances across traditional borders and wars within them. A communications revolution has brought about unlikely networks among geographically far-flung interlocutors, undermined the ability of governments to regulate or monopolize news, and at the same time provided new tools to propagandize and influence the masses. Global warming has crowded out MIRVs [multiple intercontinental reentry vehicles] and the like as the new strategic threat. Government computers that once modeled probable paths of nuclear fallout are now analyzing the trajectories of infectious diseases.

The demise of the "Evil Empire" was a victory more complete than any politician would have dared predict. The next generation of global threats shows it was not an unalloyed triumph. With the fall of the Berlin Wall, the dam burst and the Cold War drained away. The submerged territory that came into view was not the neatly ordered Atlantis so many had envisioned, but a low-tech swamp of nationalism, ethnic strife, regional tensions, and economic disasters. Subsequently, the high-tech, high-testosterone exhilaration of Operation Desert Storm generated unrealistic expectations about the ability of the United States to prevail decisively at low cost to itself in lives, money, and moral qualms. In this wake, Americans are gradually being confronted with the disillusioning realization that the "New Mess," while arguably less dangerous directly here at home, may not be easier to straighten up than the old one.

Foreign policy is our interaction with forces that we do not control. Flexibility is vital; changing circumstances constantly demand tactical adjustments and corrections. But low popular esteem for government hampers the conduct of foreign affairs by making people unwilling to take risks and skeptical of leaders' motives (if not competence) and by making the leaders more disposed to be led by the polls. The Vietnam War virtually bankrupted the government's moral authority and created an adversarial relationship between the people and their leaders. The corruption of the Watergate scandal was devastating to Americans' perception of their leaders and the political system. The low comedy of Monica Lewinsky seemed to have removed the last vestige of credible moral authority from the presidency. Since Jimmy Carter's candidacy in the 1976 elections, every candidate for national office has run as a supposed outsider (even "citizen" Bob Dole), promising to clean up Washington and tame the bureaucracy. Fear and loathing in Washington may be nothing new, but its intensity and pervasiveness are at a record high. Policymakers are therefore condemned to a vicious cycle in which their efforts to gain support from a skeptical public invites hype, oversimplification, and front-end compromises at the same time that the resource squeeze hampers their ability to deliver. These factors combine to diminish the odds of success for a given policy, validating the original lack of confidence.

These trends undermine public willingness to entrust government with resources, as witnessed by the atrophy of resources for conducting foreign affairs. *New York Times* columnist Thomas Friedman acidly observed that those who do not propose to dismantle the U.S. presence in the world propose merely not to pay for it. U.S. funding for international affairs—never more than the cost of a respectable weapons system at the Pentagon—dropped nearly 20 percent in real terms below the level of spending in the 1980s and is the only major category of federal spending that has undergone a real reduction since the Carter administration. These shortfalls and these attitudes undercut American leadership, capabilities, and authority.

Similarly, the technological revolution that beams world events to citizens real-time and offers a talk show (if not an entire channel) for every viewpoint has grown relentlessly, corrosively negative in its coverage of political leaders; this is one cause of the public's disgust with government. The rise of "interpretive journalism," using events and facts to illustrate and support a thesis, has crowded out news. This is attack dog, not watchdog, journalism because it flows from the ideological premise that politicians are venal, and therefore their behavior can be moderated only by fear of exposure, not by principles. This intersection of politics and media makes foreign policy a kind of chess game in three dimensions: how a given policy will affect the situation on the ground, how it will be received by the public, and how vulnerable it will make the administration to partisan attack.

Foreign policy may have always had these inherent elements, but the speed of the clock has been advanced by technology to the point that policymakers have to react in three dimensions simultaneously. Deliberative time has been greatly diminished or in some instances eliminated. Moreover, success is much less mediagenic than a catastrophe. A smoothly running policy is not front-page news, whereas failure is on the news for longer than it takes to deal with its consequences. The government's former power to explain the world to its citizens has been decimated, largely a casualty of the Vietnam War, when the media began openly to challenge the government's accounts. One result of all these trends is that a premium is placed on

"spinning"—the ability to deflect hard questions and to temporize—
an agility that has everything to do with political tactics and little to
do with geostrategy.

It would be absurd to argue that the technological media
revolution obviates the need for diplomacy. The proliferation of raw
information via CNN, faxes, or the Internet—often hopelessly com-
mingling fact, fiction, and error—has made harder and more important the traditional diplomatic task of making sense out of disparate
bits of information and recommending a course of action. The advent
of the Internet has ushered in the Era of the Update in which the premium is on getting it out, not getting it right. The surfeit of media
and intelligence data can present as formidable a threat to good policy-making as an information shortfall. While a barren landscape my
offer no clues, a cluttered arena may obscure them. Ignorance with
respect to an issue is rectified by knowledge, not simply by facts or
reports. Policymakers do not need news flashes or data points, they
need answers to the critical questions: What *really* happened? What
does it mean? What next? What should be done?

It is true that an embassy is no longer the sole, or in some cases
even the preeminent, channel of communication between nations or
governments. New conduits have opened through faxes, phones,
"hotlines," and the ease and frequency of official and private travel.
Much virtual diplomacy takes now place through press conferences
and soundbites administered by senior officials and government
spokespersons. The need for some authoritative, direct, and personal
communication via embassies is self-evident. But even beyond that,
news coverage from Washington, usually designed for the domestic
audience, cannot serve adequately as the U.S. presentation abroad of
its policies and positions. Satellite relays do not ensure that people
overseas will understand what the United States is saying or will form
acceptable conclusions about U.S. goals and motives. In an increasingly democratic post–Cold War world, support for U.S. positions
may depend a great deal on such perceptions. The tint of condescen-
sion—that America knows best—often accompanies long-distance
communication and cuts against the merits of a policy.

An American ambassador who can work the local media, intuit
the most effective line of argument, and provide a soundbite in the
local language can make an extraordinary contribution. Without that
capability, the power is lost to shape overseas public opinion or even
to defend effectively against damaging representations of America.

Capturing the high ground of local public opinion provides a huge advantage, but ceding it to others can turn a challenge into a lost cause. An ambassador can also garner the respect and trust of the foreign leaders with whom he or she regularly meets, gaining their confidence in the policies of the United States.

3

The Lone Superpower

While it is self-evident that the world is no longer bipolar in the traditional sense, does that mean it is unipolar, revolving around the sole superpower? Is it multipolar, comprised of geographic or geoeconomic blocs? Or is it somewhere in between—an asymmetrical bipolarity with a strong United States occupying one pole and the second-tier powers, including the European Union, Japan, China, and Russia, at another. Equally evident is that the United States is the world's only superpower. But what it means to be a superpower is subject to considerable debate and depends in no small measure on one's view of how the world is configured.

In conventional thinking, the main attribute of a superpower is military might. A National Defense University strategic assessment suggests that a paramount objective of the United States should be to maintain a military superiority sufficient to hedge against the potential emergence of a peer power. (This of course overlooks the prospect that a peer power could cooperate in securing outcomes that the U.S. could not achieve alone.) Post–Cold War deterrence should be aimed at forestalling such challengers not only from attacking but also from even the temptation to try to compete with the United States militarily. To the extent that it maintains credibility as an unmatchable military power with the largest inventory of advanced equipment, the best trained personnel, and unmatched strategic assets, such as transport logistics, intelligence, and communications, the United States can convince middle- and second-tier powers that there is fundamentally no point in pursuing an aggressive militarization program because the gap is simply too great to close.

The United States is already in pretty good shape on that score. By way of context, our defense budget is greater than those of the next ten largest military powers *combined* (few of whom are potential rivals anyway). The procurement budget alone ($76 billion in fiscal year 1997) is larger than the entire defense budget of any other country. For China's much-discussed military modernization program to catch up, the United States would essentially have to stand still for a decade. This is not in any way to suggest that our national security can be defined arithmetically as the differential in spending between ourselves and other nations. Obviously, the criterion for military capability must be a function of what we seek to accomplish or prevent. But clearly, potential military force is infinitely preferable and less costly than applied military force. To prevent an arms race by maintaining an unclosable lead will in the long run save money and in the meantime augment U.S. international influence.

We should be mindful of the fact that malefactors will "devolve" to techniques that render America's technological advantage less relevant, including terror, thereby circumventing U.S. military strengths, perhaps camouflaging the sponsoring state, and attacking what Arthur Schlesinger called "the vulnerability of a democracy"—its public's intolerance of risk. The arsenal of the "New Mess" can include fertilizer explosives in the parking lot of a high-rise, an antipersonnel device in a crowded public park, nerve gas in a subway, smallpox virus in an airport, or detonation of a nuclear device built with plutonium stolen (or purchased) from Russian stockpiles.

Effective peacemaking and peacekeeping interventions are invaluable to the maintenance of international order and to U.S. prestige. We are a superpower not only because we can take on all comers, but also because all can come to us to take on threats in their neighborhoods. The military capability that permits us to employ the threat, or the actual use of, force, is central to our super power. However, humiliating setbacks, such as the 1993 Somalia experience, can deal blows to that prestige and create a reverse impression of vulnerability. Even the short-term failure of air power to force Slobodan Milosevic to the bargaining table, let alone to his knees, raised questions about the effectiveness of the U.S. military, not to mention the bias toward "clean" air versus "dirty" ground action. Since the peacekeeping misadventures in Somalia, editorial pages have been filled with warnings against U.S. hyperinterventionism and the romantic pursuit of desperate causes in remote areas. Post–Vietnam America displays an extreme aversion to risk-taking in foreign affairs, scathingly noted by a British analyst who wrote, "For a gun-loving society prepared to tolerate mayhem and death on its streets, America's reluctance to use military force, as epitomized by its experience in Somalia and its hesitancy to send troops to Bosnia, is a serious reason to doubt the credibility of American power."

The aversion to exposing American troops to danger has intensified to the point where foreign operations are high-altitude, narrowly circumscribed affairs, creating in the extreme the appearance of peacekeeping as a public relations exercise. Perhaps as a press-induced political phenomenon in criticism-avoidance, Americans have developed a lower tolerance for casualties among professional soldiers than among inner-city children or holiday drivers. Ironically, the solicitousness toward the welfare of professional soldiers does not seem to apply to diplomats, who are routinely exposed to danger with notably higher casualties than their officer counterparts in the armed services. The realpolitik of trading soldiers' lives for limited political objectives is anathema. It is difficult enough to motivate people to accept losses in a total war against an aggressor where the objective is usually clear and the morale is normally high. The unpopularity of the Korean and Vietnam Wars directly related to the accumulation of casualties. It stands to reason, therefore, that there will be an even lower tolerance for risk in low-adrenaline, low-patriotism undertakings such as peacekeeping.

Another traditional attribute of the superpower is economic might. Has the global economy mooted the very idea of a superpower? Or have we entered the era of "economic superpowers?" It is fair to say that financial deregulation, huge money markets, trade liberalization, computerization, development of the World Trade Organization, and other multilateral factors, along with the explosive growth of large multinational firms, mean that nations cannot be said to truly control their economies? It has been suggested that international economic and financial integration and interdependence will lead to a new, non-national organization of a borderless world. And yet there is clearly the potential for a flow from Cold War to trade war. Plenty of people now define "enemies" in zero-sum commercial terms and attempt to use economic nationalism as the rallying point for the post–Cold War. Without denigrating the significance of the changes in the world economy, my own view is that the dogma of the new globalist geoeconomy is no more satisfying than the old Marxist one.

The world is not just a market, and financial and trade policies are not foreign policy. Since international economics is rooted in the international political order, a dogma that posits the primacy of geo-economics strikes me as logically flawed.

Economic strength is both a category of, and a tool of, power. In the category of economic power, the U.S. is flush. We are approaching a decade of economic expansion with nearly full employment, negligible inflation, a federal budget surplus, a soaring stock market, high international competitiveness, and a proven immunity to the "Asian financial flu." We have emerged as the world's premier economic engine, stabilizer, and lender. As a measure of power, a 1998 survey found the public (63 percent) and the foreign policy elite (89 percent) rated economic strength as more important than military strength in determining a country's overall power and influence in the world. And it is true that as a practical instrument of power, our economy gives significant direct influence. This is visible in terms of the policies of the international financial institutions that have weighted voting procedures that favor large economies, and in our ability (albeit less than complete) to use unilateral economic sanctions as a formidable threat or weapon. Just as important is the "soft power"—the prestige and stature—that flows from the size, strength, and resilience of the U.S. economy.

A digression: ironically, our parsimony toward spending in international affairs partly neutralizes the practical applicability of our extraordinary wealth. By every index, real funding for our nonmilitary conduct of international affairs has declined from a modest base and is decidedly inadequate for the challenges that come flying at us and the opportunities that go flying by us. Even the meager funding allocated to international affairs is often constrained by congressional earmarks or reallocated from crisis to crisis. The administration's inability to ante up can be a huge liability, not only undercutting our superpower image, but also creating very real problems—at the U.N., on the Korean Peninsula, and even in our ability to host major diplomatic negotiations. It could over time reduce our economic prevalence and military advantage through loss of influence.

The case for adequate resources in foreign affairs tends to be dismissed as special pleading when it comes from Foreign Service officers or State Department officials. Dozens of reports of the think tanks and scores of op ed pieces document the funding shortfall for international affairs. According to the Office of Management and

Budget's annual report, the U.S. government in 1998 spent $14.5 billion on "international affairs," $3.9 billion of which is labeled "Conduct of Foreign Affairs." Leafing through the report in search of comparable budget items reveals that we spent roughly the same amount on foreign affairs as on military family housing and on recreational resources in national parks. The same Office of Management and Budget report documents the 1998 outlay by department. The State Department's $5.2 billion compares favorably with the $4 billion spent by the Army Corps of Engineers, even if it is only a tenth of the Department of Agriculture. The disparity between our investment in military operations and in development points to a pernicious and unintended trend in which the U.S. provides the guns and planes, and others provide the reconstruction and development.

"Deadbeat" and "piker" might be the sobriquets by which we are known abroad, but America is rich—very rich. Whether we use it effectively or not, our wealth constitutes the significant "soft power" of prestige. This is manifest in the loss of influence that accompanies financial adversity. A case in point is the abrupt mooting of the "Asian values" argument, which collapsed in 1998 with the Malaysian ringghit (currency). Was it not Balzac who wrote of success that it is not enough that a man may succeed; his best friend must fail? The perturbation and defensiveness that Americans manifested in regard to the phenomenal growth of the Asian Tigers and the inexorable expansion of Japanese economic power through the mid-1990s is matched only by the triumphalism and sense of moral vindication that greeted their downfall. Declinism was rampant in the U.S. when our competitors appeared to be narrowing the gap—even though the strength of their economies brought practical benefits to the American investor and manufacturer. Now that the adrenaline has subsided after the frightening wave of bankruptcies that threatened to engulf us, one can hear voices as from the Gilded Age observing that those nouveaux riches arrivistes have at last gotten their comeuppance. Let us hope this success does not lend encouragement to the cause of isolationism.

Thomas Friedman and others have characterized fin de siècle America as "fat, dumb and happy." It is tempting to believe that, tied to that sense of economic well-being is the paradox that, despite the proliferation, activism, and influence of special interest groups, the public at large seems content in many respects to give its foreign policy proxy to the administration. If so, that would argue—ironically—

that when times are bad, people are too busy trying to make ends meet to worry much about the affairs of the world, and when times are good, they are prepared to forgo the honor. Despite the profound significance of economic strength, both practical and optical, one need look no further than the case of Japan to ascertain that wealth is not the basis for world leadership. In other words, America can be the richest burgher in the global village, but we will not lead others on that basis.

4

Leadership

America's leadership role is often characterized by Americans with a tinge of noblesse oblige—as an obligation that falls to us because no one else is capable and that we discharge with a certain grudging philanthropy. This mindset invites hubris, fosters absolutism, and contributes to the fallacy of leadership as a burden. Needless to say, it is only the burdens that Americans would like to divest themselves of, not the benefits. Being a superpower is a very good deal indeed; check with Moscow if you are not sure. Leadership brings immense, often decisive, influence; it entitles us to an opinion on every subject, guarantees that opinion will be heard, and improves the likelihood that it will be heeded. It globalizes the U.S. agenda by encouraging support for and discouraging opposition to American principles. It induces others to do things voluntarily that U.S. leaders might not have thought to ask or have succeeded in obtaining. It helps give the United States control in matters of great importance to it. It stabilizes the world on U.S. terms.

It is easy, however, to confuse strength with leadership, but military or economic predominance does not make a leader—followers do. No person or nation can attract followers without ideas, energy, and the ability to communicate. The authority of a leader—as distinct from a tyrant—comes from the ability to obtain compliance without using power. A leader makes others want to follow by reference to a principle or a plan based on values or goals they embrace. It is no surprise, therefore, nor is it "disloyal," when U.S. allies balk at following a policy that in their view contravenes the general good and is driven solely by our internal considerations or immediate advantage. (The Helms-Burton legislation on investment in Cuba and U.S. claims to a right of extraterritoriality in apprehending suspected criminals abroad are cases in point.)

The domestic political trends discussed earlier make it seem likely that U.S. foreign policies will increasingly be influenced by single-issue pressure groups. While diplomatic démarches to foreign governments have long made use of the specter of congressional pressure as a rationalization for a policy, it is doubtful that the United States has ever been as brazen as we are today in pointing to our internal political landscape, rather than the nobility of our purpose, as the primary explanation for what we are doing. Lester Thurow observes that if a leader is so weak that it cannot set aside its own interests and advocate policies that are in the general good, even if not to its own immediate advantage, and cannot therefore serve as the role model for others, it cannot lead. The reasoning is not disqualification from leadership in the abstract, but simply because others will not follow.

Unilateralism can be construed either as the need to act independently and alone, or to act exclusively on the basis of parochial self-interest. Superpower status and unilateralism might intuitively seem to go hand in hand, but in fact they are antithetical. For one thing, we have no unique national interest other than our existence as a nation—an interest that is not in jeopardy. In the absence of a single, self-evident mission—such as to prevent world domination by an enemy devoted to the destruction of the American way of life— our national interest is inextricably linked to our global ones. No acceptable mechanism exists for predicting how an international situation will affect U.S. interests. Arthur Schlesinger, writing about the temptation to define national interests narrowly in a confusing and anarchic world and the consequences of doing so, pointed out that if one is not prepared to act against evildoers, even if one is not the victim, then one does not have collective security.

The unilateralist disdain for the "periphery," properly defined as other people's backyards, is founded on a Wild West daydream of rugged individualists who tend to their own business but, in times of peril, gather a posse and bring miscreants to quick justice. But as Charles William Maynes wrote, unilateralism "will lead to isolationism because we will not be able to carry our allies with us. . . . There is a presumption that American leadership will be indefinitely sustained because of the automatic followership of our allies. But they followed because they were frightened of the Soviet Union." Put another way, if Americans define what we will do for the world strictly in terms of narrow self-interest, there is not going to be any posse when we want to go after the bad guys.

By the same token, the "lone superpower" cannot function like the "Lone Ranger." Unilateralism in the sense of acting alone, while always an option, invites the coalescence of opposing blocs uniting in a spirit of equilibrium against American hegemony. History is replete with dominant powers that spawned coalitions to oppose them and their policies. It is entirely within our power to replicate that pattern through unilateralism, and there are plenty of analysts who maintain that the administration is doing an excellent job of it. It is widely noted that the United States is acquiring a greater reputation for arrogance and hectoring since the end of the Cold War. However, the push to offset American dominion is still at the rhetorical stage. The aggregation of the European Union and of the Association of South East Asian Nations (ASEAN) represents continuity along a trajectory that was set during the Cold War and is driven largely by economic factors. To the extent that Asian nations are induced by geopolitical concerns to draw together more closely, it is in response to China, not in opposition to the United States to whom they routinely have turned for help. We have always encouraged European unity, even if we have disliked some of the European Union's trade practices. And while the Non-Aligned Movement continues to exist, it survives as a fractured amalgam of regional, religious, and ethnic groups whose agenda increasingly favors developmental issues over political ones.

A case is sometimes made in favor of a trend toward multipolarity on the concept of "benign spheres of influence"—i.e., the notion that like-minded nations will tend of their own accord to sort out problems in their own neighborhoods or that regional powers should take care of maintaining order. The problem with that contention, which is essentially feudalism for the twenty-first century, is that the regional influence exercised will not be benign, that states who would welcome (or at least tolerate) the intercession by the U.S. will vigorously resist the intervention by ambitious, partisan, and partial local powers, and that the United States will quickly find itself walled out of the spheres. It is one thing to accord more power to regional *groups*—which actually are strengthened by the degree to which the United States participates in or engages in them. It is altogether another thing to defer to regional *powers* whose neighbors are not interested in seeing them become hegemons, for reasons of history, sovereignty, and even national survival. Is Asia prepared to accord to China the role of regional broker? South Asia, India? Latin America, Brazil? The noteworthy fact is that, notwithstanding protests over night landing practice and the other inconveniences of hosting a U.S. military base, the countries of other regions desire a significant U.S. presence precisely to *prevent* regional powers from trapping them in a sphere of influence. Furthermore, the notion that we could tolerate an international system of regional jurisdiction—a kind of warlord-ism—is at odds with the effect of an emergent American multicultural trend in which the interests of disparate groups and countries are championed (or contested) in Washington.

Multilateral diplomacy is routinely dismissed as a kind of naiveté; yet the adroit practitioners of multilateral diplomacy—Singapore's agility at the UN and in ASEAN springs to mind—are able to exert influence vastly beyond their ostensible national capacities. More importantly, the products of multilateral diplomacy are of immense practical consequence: indefinite extension of the Nuclear Nonproliferation Treaty; bringing into force the Comprehensive Test Ban Treaty; ratification of the Chemical Weapons Convention; strengthening the Biological Weapons Convention and the Missile Technology Control Regime; and creation of the International War Crimes Tribunal. To these are added ecological agreements, trade and commercial arrangements, a land-mine regime (like it or not), and other measures covering global threats such as infectious disease, narcotics, terrorism, and crime. These treaties, conventions, and institutions in many cases codify U.S. military superiority, curtail potential challenges, and diminish the likelihood of threats to U.S. security. This is the immeasurable value of multilateral diplomacy.

Working with and through international organizations can offer advantages both as a power multiplier (since risks, costs, resources, and capabilities are all shared) and as behavior modifier (since the institutions and their members promote and reinforce global rules and norms). Multilateral efforts enable us to do more for less. The United States has traditionally wielded immense behind-the-scenes influence, permitting us to affect circumstances and influence the behavior of others without direct bilateral confrontations and consequences. International organizations are not constituted for the purpose of according the United States an advantage over others; they protect American interests although they will not necessarily favor them. We can shape, although not dictate, the agenda and implement it at a far lower cost and risk, which is apportioned—sometimes on an inequitable basis extremely favorable to us—among member states. U.S. influence in key institutions (e.g., the UN Security Council, NATO, the IMF) far exceeds our actual contributions in money and manpower. Deft diplomacy can enhance that ratio further. Moreover, active international organizations and regional groups improve the chances of finding early solutions to problems at the regional level, thus diminishing the likelihood that direct U.S. intervention will be required. In a similar vein, institutions such as the World Trade Organization, the International War Crimes Tribunal, the International Court of Justice, the International Atomic Energy Association, the UN Human Rights Commission, the IMF, and dozens of other organizations have created a network of rules, conventions, and adjudication processes that do much to stem, reveal, or punish misbehavior. By setting standards accepted by the preponderance of nations, they work counter to the ancient precept that a nation is entitled to all it can get away with. They can provide authoritative reprimands for violations, although they can be no more effective in commanding obedience or at punishing malfeasance than their members' will or capabilities allow.

The United States has every interest in maximizing respect for and adherence to international rules, since it has the most to protect with these rules and, in fact, makes most of them. As the dominant rule setter, the U.S.'s behavior is closely measured against the standards it sets for others. We cannot lead by bad example; misdemeanors will beget others' felonies. Rejection of verdicts rendered by the International Court of Justice or failure to ratify key international conventions can only beget similar behavior elsewhere. Already, for instance, nonpayment of debt has mushroomed in the UN system, with dozens of countries in arrears where virtually none stood before the Reagan administration. U.S. nonpayment has created a shortfall that weakens the United Nations and provides fodder for our critics. The UN in turn has an interest in seeing that the "pain" of the U.S. default is felt by member states (e.g., by nonpayment of peacekeeping reimbursements) to generate political pressure on Washington. The United States has become a target of resentment and, worse, ridicule. Our continued claim to be withholding funds pending satisfactory administrative reform—as opposed to simply welshing on a debt—is derided by most other nations. The damaging perception is of an arrogant bully who does not play by the rules because it cannot win by the rules. As the U.S. sours on the UN, the UN sours on us. For most other nations, multilateral diplomacy is the fast track that takes professional diplomats to the top of their service and on which important political actors frequently take a turn. American contempt for the UN is acutely insulting to tomorrow's foreign ministers and prime ministers. By disenfranchising other nations through unilateralism, the U.S. helps to unite them against us. If we are not a constructive party to international deliberations, we can easily become the object of them. Given the size, strength, and wealth of the United States, we will always be central to multilateral diplomacy, either as a leader or a target.

5
Order Maintenance

National interest is not like pornography; one does *not* necessarily know it when one sees it. In fact, when one reviews the events leading to crises, it is humbling to note how little we knew about what was to follow. It is axiomatic that huge changes turn on small events. Thus the fundamental inadequacy of the proposition that the United States can downsize its foreign policy to concentrate on the "really important" things is the unreliability of ascertaining which things will really be important in the long run. Also, the bias in favor of concentrating on serious problems guarantees a steady supply of them because they are less likely to be solved in their formative stages or to be prevented.

By the time that a threat to our national security and interests is self-evident, it is already too late. American self-absorption or poor stewardship on the international scene can restore in the twenty-first century the "them-vs.-us" clarity of the twentieth by permitting the emergence of a new Hitler or a new "Evil Empire." On the other hand, America could certainly dissipate its national energy, treasure, and consensus by the indiscriminate search abroad for incipient monsters to destroy—particularly if the monster (for instance a Somali warlord) manages to elude and even humiliate us. No foreign policy technicians in lab coats could have told us that the emerging preeminence of a relatively minor nationalistic Serb leader in Belgrade would precipitate a series of crises that would directly challenge American world leadership, imperil the NATO alliance, call into question the role of the UN Security Council, and jeopardize the West's ties with Moscow.

Former Defense Secretary William Perry advocated the doctrine "prevent, deter, defeat." His thesis was that managing conflict in the post–Cold War security environment rests on three basic lines of defense: "The first line is to prevent threats from emerging; the second is to deter threats that do emerge; and the third, if prevention and deterrence fail, is to defeat the threat using military force." Preventive diplomacy is a much-analyzed doctrine; traditionally it means averting the development of specific problems through intervention at an early stage. But it can also mean creating an environment that is less likely to foster problems. The latter category particularly warrants a closer look.

Fifteen years ago, an article entitled "Broken Windows" appeared in the *Atlantic Monthly.* It was written by two criminologists who described the relationship between public disorder and serious crime. Recently, a new book by one of the authors returns to this thesis and expands upon it. The basic premise is that order begets order and disorder begets chaos. For example, a broken window in a factory will lead passersby to form an impression that the building is decaying and not worth protecting or repairing in the eyes of its owners and the community. If it goes unrepaired, eventually someone will throw rocks at another window. Multiple broken windows will promote the impression that the street is unsupervised and in fact dangerous. Soon, people will begin avoiding the street; local business will be hurt and perhaps shops will close, fulfilling the impression of decay. In other words, small disorders lead inexorably to larger ones.

This construct is at bottom recognition of the fact that rules are self-reinforcing; the more often and brazenly they are broken, the easier it is to ignore them. Conversely, the incongruity of misbehavior in a well-regulated universe draws attention and censure that tends to inhibit all but the sociopath. The object of order maintenance is not to counter the sociopath, but to strengthen the inhibitions of the majority. Problems in a system are manageable as long as they are addressed regularly and early. When left untreated, they can attain critical proportions and become uncontrollable, sometimes despite the most aggressive treatment. This "disorder threshold," or what epidemiologists call the "tipping point," is what distinguishes an outbreak from an epidemic or a demonstration from a riot.

The analogy between maintenance of world and civic order, while not perfect, is not frivolous. Theodore Roosevelt (who gained political prominence as a New York police commissioner), issued the famous call for the United States to exercise police power (in the Western Hemisphere) since "chronic wrongdoing or an impotence which results in the loosening of ties of civilized society may . . . ultimately require intervention by some civilized nation."

While Roosevelt advocated the connection, George Kennan lamented it. He decried the "fallacy that America has a measure of responsibility for everything that happens [in the world] even if only from faint-heartedness and poor judgment if not outright treason." He called on his compatriots to "recognize that there are problems in this world that we will not be able to solve, depths into which it will not be useful or effective for us to plunge, dilemmas in other regions of the globe that will have to find their solution without our involvement."

Walter Lippman wrote in 1965 that "the U.S. did not intervene in Tibet for the good and sufficient reason that the U.S. could not reach Tibet in order to defend it."

Roosevelt's point was not about the ethics or the logistics of intervention. His concept was that America's stake in the world (even though his world was essentially the Western Hemisphere) gives the United States a material interest in seeing to it that chronic problems do not go untreated because of the consequences for the United States if they do. It is not hard to make the connection between order maintenance in the community and in the world.

This does not mean that America should be the world's policeman. It does signify, however, that America can only flourish in a largely law-abiding world. The reason is simply that we have so much to lose. No nation past or present is as rich as the United States is today, thanks to our phenomenal natural resources and immensely successful political, economic, and social strategies. As Bob Koehene put it, "America was not only born free, it was born lucky." Notwithstanding the challenges we face, the world is largely conducive to fundamental American interests. Riddled as it is with pitfalls and dangers, international society is dominated by a congenial international order and is marked by the growth of freedom and democracy, acknowledgment of human rights, acceptance of the need to conserve environmental resources, and growth of the free market capitalist economic system. Added to this, Americans today enjoy secure borders and strong national prestige.

U.S. policies should be oriented toward the preservation of this favorable climate and these healthy trends. No nation has as much to lose. The United States is the largest holder of equity in the planet; it is axiomatic that this gives it the greatest stake in the world's equilibrium and well-being. This is not to suggest the preservation of the structure of the world, problems and all, or to imply an aversion to change. The point is that American interests are served by stability and by the effective operation of the system that has allowed the United States to preserve and increase its wealth, develop its potential, and improve the lives and welfare of its citizens. It would be a mistake to think that the U.S.'s huge equity in the world argues for stasis; Americans benefit immensely from economic, technological, and other forms of growth, as the past decade abundantly attests, and have the most to lose from stagnation. But change, to be manageable and beneficial to U.S. interests, must occur within a framework that maintains the positive attributes and structures of the world. In other words, the United States needs a world that operates by the rules.

A system that encourages and rewards compliance in modes of international behavior is every bit as important as one that retaliates against severe violations of international law. The applicability of the "broken windows" theorem is that a breakdown of order in a given part of the world, if left unaddressed, will eventually contribute to the erosion of confidence in the prevailing norms and mores, thus engendering the cynicism and contempt for rules and conventions, and thereby fostering challenges to established order elsewhere. The failure of leading nations, individually or collectively, to respond to problems and challenges generates the perception that they are incapable of doing so. This perception is an invitation to larger problems.

Because of our strength and preeminence, the United States is the dominant rule setter with respect to the basic norms of international conduct. We ask (and sometimes force) other nations to play by our rules—in trade, in political affairs, in security issues, on human rights, and in most other respects. This dominance means that, in effect, an attack on the world system of rules is an attack on the United States; deviation from the norms is in some respects defiance of the United States. Sometimes the defiance is explicit: acts of terror against the "Great Satan" or military threats to a U.S. ally. However, festering problems, even in regions of no obvious strategic value, should also be understood as serious challenges to the geopolitical ecosystem and therefore to U.S. well-being. To signal an unwillingness or an inability to deal with them undermines our moral authority and political influence. Conversely, the perception that leaders—on a local or global scale—understand a problem, care about it, and are "doing something" enhances the effectiveness of the leaders, in part by creating a presumption of eventual success. The difference does not necessarily hinge on whether the problems are actually solved (most problems are not). In terms of order maintenance, the critical element is faith in the leadership's *ability* and *determination* to solve or at least to control problems.

The world needs an energizing force to overcome the sense that problems are intractable, since that perception fosters cynicism and encourages the resort to power politics. The ability to galvanize individuals into community action by inculcating a sense of confidence and of purpose is crucial. John Ikenberry wrote that the "heroic" American leadership of an earlier era has been reinvented in the form of a dense set of transnational linkages and can long outlast the decline of its postwar position of absolute dominance or the stumbling of a particular administration. This theory goes far beyond the old hegemony of the strong; it implies institutional leadership that establishes rules, and expectations that facilitate concerted action and that induce others to accept constraints necessary to advance common interests.

The concept of order maintenance is at odds with two mainstream theories in international affairs. The first is that the United States can benignly neglect the problems of the world that do not constitute existential threats to the U.S. and our way of life. The second posits the existence of a foreign policy paradigm that would structure our policy-making with the elegance and authority that Einstein's $e = mc^2$ formula lends to physics. But order maintenance itself faces the conundrum of how to decide where we invest our efforts, since we cannot be everywhere and do everything. There is an often-cited risk of promiscuous intervention that America cannot afford. No one would disagree that meddling, liberal guilt, and evangelism are impulses that should not guide American foreign policy. There is also the risk of an ethnocentric or even racist double standard of intervention. After all, this nation mobilized formidable resources to address ethnic cleansing and mass expulsions in the Balkans; why could we not do as much for the vastly larger tragedy in the Great Lakes region of Africa? Similarly, by what means do we decide whether to champion an international coalition to respond to ethnic or religious strife within the borders of a sovereign state when there are major implications for regional stability? (In the case of the former Yugoslavia, we did; in the case of Indonesia, we did not.) How is it that we mobilized the UN Security Council and ultimately sent warships to compel foreign military leaders to honor the outcome of national elections in Haiti but not in Nigeria or Burma?

Consonant with the premise of "Broken Windows" is a mix of factors that drive the natural selection by which we choose (or are impelled) to intervene abroad. They can be sketched out along the following lines:

Strategic: The U.S. government in fact has a broad set of defined international strategic goals, coordinated among the various foreign affairs agencies and updated annually. This constitutes a useful set of references covering the spectrum of our key interests that helps to harmonize the work of the executive branch actors. Beginning—naturally—with direct and potential military threats, the document defines key U.S. interests as promoting economic prosperity, safeguarding U.S. citizens and borders; enforcing transnational law (e.g., narcotics and terrorism); promoting values (democracy, good governance, and human rights); responding to humanitarian disasters; and safeguarding the planet from global threats (e.g., environmental, infectious diseases, etc.).

Political: In international terms, threats to the interests of close allies ineluctably become our problem, often for reasons of economic or historical importance. On the domestic side, as described earlier, America has a largely self-correcting political system that, while imperfect, serves to negotiate priorities among competing interest groups, examine and debate options, lobby or protest, modulate extremism, and—thanks in no small measure to an aggressive media—to leave no significant foreign policy decision unchallenged. This includes the influential foreign policy elites as well as NGOs. In terms of traditional domestic politics, many an administration has been hoist on the petard of its own campaign pledges about actions it would take, thereby preempting or preordaining certain policy choices.

Credo: Commingled with the U.S. political system is a dynamic but largely coherent set of American values. These include historical, economic, cultural, ethical, social, and other biases and traditions that influence decisions about whether and how we should involve ourselves in the affairs of the world.

Practical: There are pragmatic or common sense considerations that set priorities and shape decisions. Loose nukes will always take precedence over loose muskets. Sudden instability in a traditionally healthy region with significant economic ties to the U.S. will loom larger than chronic instability in remote arenas with a history of disorder where intervention is logistically difficult.

Professional: Last (but not least) is the role played by the professional foreign policy cadres who can influence decisions about American intervention or engagement. They are charged with tracking and making sense of events, formulating plans and options, carrying out policies, and advancing America's values and interests.

It is this mix of factors that does and will serve as the regulator on our foreign policy-making. We should accept, not decry, the operation of "rational prioritizing," while facing up to the challenge of reconciling the contradictory impulses of our multicultural and information-rich society. The trick, of course, is to get the right mix. Giving short shrift to one factor, or exaggerating the sway of another, is certain to create defects in the formulation or the implementation of the policy. That is the flaw in the theory that the key to good foreign policy lies simply in "leaving it to the experts." Quite apart from the certainty that political factors will inevitably intrude, professional advice, whether on Wall Street or Foggy Bottom, can be vague, contradictory, or—let us face it—just plain wrong. But this is not to suggest that expertise is unavailing in foreign affairs. It is as crucial as in other disciplines such as medicine, finance, and the law. We are foolish to make decisions without reference to professional expertise or to ignore the advice that we get. The key is in balance. To put it another way, the sway of politics over diplomacy is akin to civilian control of the military—too little invites bad decisions, too much invites calamities

6
Conclusion

No nation is so strong that it can afford not to be smart in its dealings with the world.

"Bright" makes right more effectively than does might—and usually makes it without a fight! Key to getting it "right" in international affairs is a healthy balance between the policy establishment (reflecting the political aims, concerns, and circumstances of the nation) and the foreign affairs professionals. The basic canons of success are not unique to foreign policy: clarity in terms of what one is setting out to accomplish; persuasion and inclusiveness in bringing the necessary constituencies along; effectiveness in designing and executing the mission plan (including freedom from arbitrary interference); and adequacy of resources.

Bringing clarity to U.S. goals in international affairs is generally held to be a prerequisite to success, and personal experience in government supports that thesis. Of course clarity alone is insufficient; history has demonstrated that an entire nation can launch itself with singleness of purpose toward a disastrous objective. Moreover, the clarity of dogma is clearly not what we are striving for. In essence, the key is avoiding confusion about our purposes and goals in order that we may be more effective in realizing them.

The second necessary element is forging at least a core consensus in support of a policy. Except for rare moments of high passion in a nation's life that unite the people in a single purpose, there must be a process of political discussion to produce the shared definition of objectives necessary to galvanize the people. Leadership is vital to building a consensus but it is inadequate as a prescription since it cannot be dispensed. The alchemy of political leadership is comprised of an unknowable ratio of core ingredients, including strong convictions, persuasiveness, a reliable assessment of public opinion, probably a healthy measure of tactical skill, and a willingness to judge and to take some element of risk at critical times. Great leaders have been deemed great precisely because they found ways to reconcile competing imperatives and to articulate goals that were both inspirational and attainable.

The third element—the design and the execution of foreign policy—represents the critical intersection between the political leadership and the professional cadres. The payoff for an equipped, configured, and trained diplomatic corps comes in the actual management of real-world situations. Beyond overseeing the traditional bilateral diplomatic missions, U.S. policymakers need to influence the transnational aspects of international affairs that Americans say they care about—job protection, drug flow, and weapons of mass destruction. The Cold War presented the formidable challenge of analyzing the intentions and actions of one opponent, but it also enabled the United States more easily to understand (or to ignore) those of third countries that could be expected largely to follow in the U.S. or Soviet wake. Now the United States must apply itself to the task of accurately assessing friends and potential challengers as well as designing effective strategies for influencing their behavior. Not only have many countries lost Cold War inhibitions about criticizing the United States, but also some are now predisposed to test and, in some cases, challenge us.

The calculus is straightforward. The United States wants to influence the behavior of other governments (and regional groups). In order to have a calibrated effect on their policies and avoid unintended effects (such as nationalistic backlash), policymakers must have a sound understanding of their political psychology. In addition, particularly with powers such as China and Russia, the United States needs to have significant areas of constructive governmental interaction to ensure that no single issue or controversy monopolizes the bilateral relationship. This requires substantive contact involving a broad range of issues, otherwise the relationship will be marked by bursts of intense intervention in specific areas of concern, leaving scars and seldom achieving lasting results.

Never has the game been more complex. The new tools of coercion such as war crimes tribunals and economic sanctions require special skills in design and execution. Even when successfully inaugurated, they can be undermined by negative media coverage of collateral damage from sanctions on innocent populations. The growth of such factors and actors as ethnic chauvinism, regional polarization, and the role of multilateral institutions, nongovernmental organizations, and multinational corporations further increases the demands on U.S. diplomatic skills. At the same time, the Cold War primacy of security considerations has yielded to a basket of global issues that involve many diverse players. Instead of exclusive dealings with the host country's foreign ministry, American diplomats may find themselves obliged to deal with a Ministry of Trade and Industry, local industry, interest groups, media, labor unions, representatives of international specialized agencies, and in-country representatives of American businesses and advocacy groups.

Just as we need equilibrium in the political-professional nexus, we need balance in the actual practice of foreign policy-making. There is often a tug-of-war between grand strategy on the one hand and "ad hocery" on the other. The ratio traditionally slides steadily from the former to the latter through the life cycle of an administration. It is human nature to believe that a set of guiding principles will enable us to navigate world events by delineating priorities. To set priorities is admirable and essential but must not be confused with the dynamic operation of real-world *prioritizing*. The world will always conspire to throw a curveball. The most sagacious theory and ingenious paradigm will be tucked into a back pocket as a stream of challenges forces itself upon policymakers, who must confront the fact that prioritization is often a series of Hobson's choices between terrible alternatives. This is not to downplay the importance of guiding principles; without a considered set of abiding objectives and specific goals, we are floundering, not functioning. But the gravity of grand principles must be mated with the agility of astute tactics in order to deal with the real world.

Crises cannot be ignored, but they can be contained and in many cases averted. "An ounce of prevention" is an old bromide, and the doctrine of crisis prevention has frequently been oversold. Preventative diplomacy will not eradicate conflicts like the World Health Organization eradicated smallpox. By the same token, an expert diplomatic service will not be able to prevent or even predict all problems, but it will certainly help policymakers to make better choices earlier and to be more effective in implementing policies to deal with problems that could not be averted.

The world's problems are seldom secret. Much of international affairs is dealing with chronic or predictable disputes. In many cases, the goal is to dampen and contain conflicts at a level safely removed from violence. To be effective, we must draw on a universe of conventional and unconventional strategies, including nongovernmental, track-two efforts, observer missions, targeted economic aid, confidence-building measures, the good offices of international organizations, democracy building, mediation, economic sanctions, and good old-fashioned pressure. The better our reconnaissance and delivery vehicle—i.e., the diplomatic operation—the better the chances of success. It is that simple.

Nothing in the principle of order maintenance calls for utopian crusades or promiscuous intervention. U.S. foreign policy must be conducted within our means, and international missions must have realistic prospects for success. But failure to invest adequately in the foreign affairs infrastructure will simply assure that U.S. intervention will come late and will be hobbled by inadequacies of information, analysis, and action. It is imperative that we allocate resources to ensure we are adequately provisioned, staffed, trained, and prepared to contend with the unwelcome, the unexpected, and the unruly mischief of a turbulent world.

Ultimately, it is not enough for the United States to be strong in any of the indexes of power. We have to be well organized and smart. We need a purposeful foreign policy that aims at a world we can agreeably live in and the resourcefulness to find methods to that end that are not self-defeating. The overpowering interest of the United States rests in using our wiles, wealth, and wisdom to create and preserve a peaceful world congenial to our values.

About the Author

Daniel Russel is a career Foreign Service officer who has served in Japan, Korea, Cyprus, the United Nations, and Washington where he was Special Assistant and later Chief of Staff to the Under Secretary for Political Affairs. He attended Sarah Lawrence College and the University of London, where he studied Philosophy. Before joining the State Department he achieved a black belt in Aikido and spent six years in private industry in New York City.